Past   Present

YAKIMA

ON THE OPPOSITE PAGE: In 1908, the North Yakima Steam Dyeing & Cleaning Works Company was located at 108 North 1st Street, on the west side of North 1st Street north of East A Street (now Staff Sgt. Pendleton Way). At the time this photograph was taken, the company was owned by Joseph E. LaFreniere. Today, the site is a parking lot just south of the Yakima County Jail. (Courtesy of Dale Renney and Yakima Valley Museum.)

PAST   PRESENT

YAKIMA

Ellen Allmendinger

To Yakima history lovers who enjoy remembering Yakima's past.

Copyright © 2022 by Ellen Allmendinger
ISBN 978-1-4671-0812-6

Library of Congress Control Number: 2022930631

Published by Arcadia Publishing
Charleston, South Carolina

Printed in the United States of America

For all general information, please contact Arcadia Publishing:
Telephone 843-853-2070
Fax 843-853-0044
E-mail sales@arcadiapublishing.com
For customer service and orders:
Toll-Free 1-888-313-2665

Visit us on the Internet at www.arcadiapublishing.com

On the Front Cover: A post-1907 trolley travels west on East Yakima Avenue at Front Street. The Hotel Washington and the Alfalfa Saloon (in the Lund Building) are shown on the left, and the Panama and Empire Hotels are on the right. Of those noted, only the Lund Building remains standing today. (Past image, courtesy of Yakima Valley Museum; present image, photograph by the author.)

On the Back Cover: A circus parade heads east on East Yakima Avenue in 1901. Several circuses arrived in the city during its early years, with parades down East Yakima Avenue as part of the show. (Photograph by Frank P. Lanterman; courtesy of Yakima Valley Museum.)

Contents

Acknowledgments		vii
Introduction		ix
1.	Street Scenes	11
2.	Theaters	53
3.	Courthouses	61
4.	Fire Stations	71
5.	Hotels	75
6.	Train Depots	89

Acknowledgments

This book would not have been possible without the assistance of those who provided the opportunity, historical photographs, information, and personal support during the process of putting it all together from conception to publication.

I am indebted to Arcadia Publishing for the company's trust in requesting that I compile this book and Arcadia's wonderful staff, who patiently guided me through the process.

Without the assistance provided by John Baule and the Yakima Valley Museum and Archives, it would have been impossible to complete this project. Their tireless work to preserve Yakima's history and provide information for publication is what ultimately made this work possible.

A huge thanks to my son Zakary Allmendinger, once again, for exercising patience a third time while I worked to complete this book.

Gratitude is also owed to John Dykes for his unconditional and continual moral support throughout the entire process of this project.

Last but not least, to Yakima's history lovers who have graciously supported my research, tours, and previous books in the name of sharing history, your enduring enthusiasm to learn more about our local history is what keeps me motivated.

Unless noted otherwise, all past photographs appear courtesy of Yakima Valley Museum. The present-day images are by Ellen Allmendinger.

Introduction

In 1884, Yakima, Washington (initially North Yakima), began as a high desert, sagebrush-filled townsite with a makeshift railroad boxcar serving as a train depot. Within a year of the city being platted, over 100 buildings had been relocated to the new townsite. Over the next decade, the number of businesses, buildings, and people in Yakima exploded, making it one of the largest cities in Central Washington.

The economic success and growth of Yakima continued for over half a century. Buildings were continuously being constructed and filled with government and municipal functions as well as private enterprises. Merchants flourished while the city streets were often crowded with citizens and visitors shopping or conducting business. Large gatherings were frequently held in the city's streets to pay tribute to prominent visiting public figures or participate in celebrations and entertainment.

As the 1960s arrived, Yakima was not excluded from the various economic changes that impacted the rest of the region. Several of the city's once-thriving businesses began experiencing hardships or simply closing. The buildings that housed them began showing signs of age and decay. Several of the once prominent and fully occupied structures slowly became partially or completely vacant. As downtown properties were sold, new property owners chose to demolish the buildings that once dominated the city, often replacing them with new ones or parking lots. Sadly, this trend continued over the next 50 years despite various attempts at revitalization.

Few of the original buildings remain of those that once lined the downtown streets of the city and contained thriving businesses. With the loss of many of these structures, Yakima's business core and landscape have been significantly altered. Few visual clues remain to remind residents or visitors of the formerly bustling downtown area. Because of these losses, in part, the changes that have occurred in Yakima over the last 140 years remain unknown to most.

CHAPTER 1

STREET SCENES

By 1901, downtown North Yakima (now Yakima) had increased in size significantly. This view from the now-gone Sloan Building shows the large number of buildings that once stood in the area. The intersection of South 1st Street and East Chestnut Avenue is on the right, and the Central School is in the back. (Photograph by Frank P. Lanterman.)

The 1908 photograph below looks south in Railway Park, located on the west side of North Front Street, between the third North Yakima passenger depot (in the background) and East B Street (now Martin Luther King Jr. Boulevard). With grass, a gazebo, and a fountain, the park served as a gathering place. In 1910, with the construction of the fourth North Yakima passenger depot, the park was removed. Today, the location is home to a parking lot. (Below, photograph by L.E. Smith.)

The Yakima Livery Stable was located on the northeast corner of North Front Street and East A Street (now Staff Sgt. Pendleton Way). The business had occupied the site since the beginning of North Yakima. As shown in the 1888 photograph above, the livery was owned and operated by Henry Lewis Tucker, a Civil War veteran and former Yakima County sheriff. Today, the corner lot houses part of the Yakima County Jail.

Street Scenes

The above view looks southeast on North Front Street toward East Yakima Avenue in 1886. The buildings shown were among the earliest in the city's history and were all demolished or destroyed by fire within two decades. Today, this same section of the street is the location of several of the city's oldest historic buildings, including the Sydney Hotel, North Yakima City Hall, and the Switzer Opera House.

In 1918, the inside and outside of the Switzer Opera House were used by community members as staging areas to gather and sort clothing. The clothing was ultimately shipped by train to support soldiers and others during World War I. The Switzer Opera House building still stands and is located on the east side of North Front Street, north of East Yakima Avenue.

The Twenty Millionth 1931 Ford Model A Sedan traveled across the United States in 1931–1932. While on tour, it stopped in Yakima and served as the focal point of several gatherings. In the below photograph, the sedan is surrounded by local Ford employees while parked outside the Switzer Opera House building and the Yakima Transfer & Storage Company (located within the building). Today, the Switzer Opera House building remains standing on North Front Street.

A horse-drawn wagon loaded with pipe is pictured above in 1914 outside the Redmon Steel Tube Company on North 1st Street, just north of East Yakima Avenue. The Redmon Steel Tube Company was located on the first floor of the building behind the loaded wagon. The second floor was the one-time home of the Yakima Bindery and Printing Company. The location is presently the site of a Wells Fargo Bank building and parking lot.

STREET SCENES

FIRST STREET.

These images look north on South 1st Street from just north of East Walnut Street. In the left foreground in the above image is the Pacific Hotel building located in what was once the Japan Town area of the city; in the left background is the Washington Hotel. Both establishments were competitors and considered fine hotels. Only the building that housed the Pacific Hotel still stands today. (Above, courtesy of Dale Renney and the Yakima Valley Museum.)

The Yakima Veterinary Hospital, shown below behind the horses in the street, was located at 209 South 1st Street in 1908. The building stood on the southeast corner of South 1st Street and East Chestnut Avenue. Operated by Charles A. Jones, a veterinary surgeon, the hospital was a popular clinic in the city for injured or sick horses. Today, the property is the location of the K&K Custom Furniture Store.

Street Scenes

The Yakima Hardware Company once had several buildings in the city. The 1920 photograph below shows one of the buildings that stood on the west side of South 1st Street, just north of East Spruce Street. Originally starting as Weed & Rowe Hardware on Yakima Avenue, the company became the largest hardware company in the city, with multiple buildings. Today, the structure bears little resemblance to how it looked in its early years.

Built in 1889, the Syndicate Building was once located at the southeast corner of North 2nd Street and East A Street (now Staff Sgt. Pendleton Way). At one time, the building once housed the public library and the Elks Club. In the 1908 photograph above, it was the home of Lombard-Horsley Furniture Company, as well as an undertaker, the Biochemic Remedy Company, and Dr. J.B. Chapman's office. The site is now a parking lot.

1156 – Second Street, North Yakima, Washington.

The Miller Building once dominated the northeast corner of the 2nd Street and East Yakima Avenue intersection. In the above postcard with a view from west of North 2nd Street, the building's size is evident. Today, the alignment of the once-business-lined North 2nd Street has changed dramatically. The buildings shown on the left side of the above photograph no longer exist. The street is now lined with parking lots and newer structures.

The Lewis-Engle Building was located on the southeast corner of 2nd Street and East Yakima Avenue. In the below photograph, it was home to the Pugsley Real Estate offices and a furniture store. Most will remember the building as the previous location of the popular Jade Tree Restaurant. After heavy snowfalls during the winter of 1996 resulted in damages to the building, it was demolished. Today, the site is home to Cowiche Canyon Kitchen.

Street Scenes

Below is a c. 1900 northward view of South 2nd Street from south of East Yakima Avenue. On the far right are the Miller and Lewis-Engle Buildings. The Acme Café is visible in the left foreground. In recent times, the alignment of 2nd Street and the buildings that once lined it have changed significantly. Today, the Larson Building and multiple parking lots dominate the scene.

In 1900, the Chicago Dry Goods Company was located on the west side of South 2nd Street south of East Yakima Avenue. Operated by D.A. Hannah, the company sold clothing and various other goods. In the above photograph, unidentified people are shown standing outside the company among items being sold. The building that housed the company no longer exists; it was located on the site of what is now the southeast portion of the Larson Building.

In the early 1900s, South 2nd Street was packed with buildings between East Chestnut and East Yakima Avenues. The Palace Bakery, a saddlery, cigar store, and the Centennial Hall Building are shown on the left in the above image. At right, the large Grand Hotel (later the Donnelly Hotel) is in the foreground with the Lewis-Engle and Miller Buildings behind it. Today, the Larson Building and parking lots dominate the block. (Above, photograph by Frank P. Lanterman; courtesy of the Jack Whitnall collection, Yakima Valley Museum.)

These views look north on South 2nd Street toward East Chestnut Avenue from just north of East Walnut Street. Among the buildings and businesses that occupied the block at the time of the below photograph were the Donnelly Hotel (on the right) and the Larson Building, a gas company, a cleaning company, and a radio company (on the left). Today, few of these buildings remain, and the Larson Building looms over the landscape.

STREET SCENES

The Post Office News Stand was located at the northwest corner of South 3rd Street and East Chestnut Avenue in 1910. Behind the newsstand, the back of the Donnelly Hotel (located on South 2nd Street) can be seen. Today, both the newsstand and the Donnelly Hotel are gone and have been replaced by parking lots, while the Larson Building is in the background.

The above view looks east on East Chestnut Avenue toward South 2nd Street in 1901. The federal courthouse and post office are visible in the back of the photograph. In the city's early years, the block was often filled with horses belonging to people traveling to the city. Today, a parking lot dominates the location on the left, while a parking garage is on the right. (Above, photograph by Frank P. Lanterman; courtesy of the Jack Whitnall collection, Yakima Valley Museum.)

STREET SCENES

The 1901 image above shows the north side of East Chestnut Avenue between South 1st and South 2nd Streets. The block often served as a camping and staging area for those visiting the city. It was also considered to be part of what was once the city's Chinatown. Today, the site is a parking lot. (Above, photograph by Frank P. Lanterman; courtesy of the Jack Whitnall collection, Yakima Valley Museum.)

These views look east on East Walnut Street from just west of 1st Street. In the early 1900s, the area on the left side of the below photograph served as the southern border of the city's Chinatown. In the below photograph, taken in the 1930s, the third North Yakima Fire Station is visible in the far distance, and the Wikstrom-Widener Motor Company is on the left. Today, the block looks dramatically different.

STREET SCENES

Below is a northward glimpse toward the city's fruit row vicinity on North 1st Avenue from West Yakima Avenue in 1920. To the left is a roofing company, and to the right is the Pacific Fruit & Produce Company building. Today, the roofing company building is home to Fossen's, and the warehouse on the right is home to the State of Washington Department of Ecology as well as various businesses on the first floor.

Trolley tracks are being placed at the intersection of East Yakima Avenue and Front Street in the 1907 image above. The intersection was among the first in the downtown area to have lines placed in both directions, allowing trolleys to better serve the city. The Lund Building, with the Alfalfa Saloon housed inside it, is near the back of the photograph. Today, the tracks are gone and the streets are paved.

STREET SCENES

The above image was captured during the laying of trolley tracks at the intersection of East Yakima Avenue and Front Street in 1907. At right is the northern edge of what was once the city's Japan Town, with the Empire Hotel, Yakima Lodging, and the Panama Hotel buildings visible. Today, the tracks no longer exist at this location, nor do the buildings shown at right. (Above, photograph by Olive E. Thompson.)

The Henry H. Schott Company was located on the north side of East Yakima Avenue just west of 1st Street. In the early 1907 photograph below, the outside of the business is shown with a horse-drawn roller outside. Less than a decade after this picture was taken, the Henry Schott building became part of the Washington Hotel. Today, a McDonald's occupies the location. (Below, photograph by Frank P. Lanterman.)

STREET SCENES

The Sloan Building was once located at the southwest corner of East Yakima Avenue and 1st Street within what was once the city's Japan Town. As shown in the below photograph, the building was home to the Sloan Drug Store. A doctor's and dentist's office were also located inside the building, as well as the Richelieu, a restaurant owned by the Wong family. This later became the site of the Alaskan Corral. Today, a drive-thru bank occupies the location.

This view looks east on East Yakima Avenue from 1st Street toward the intersection with 2nd Street. Above, the Yakima National Bank is in the right foreground, with First National Bank and the Lewis-Engle Building farther back on the right side. On the left side of the street, building construction is visible. The above photograph is from *Art Work on Eastern Washington and Western Idaho*, published by Charles T. Daily in 1900.

STREET SCENES 37

The Yakima National Bank, shown in the 1910 image above, once stood one lot east of the East Yakima Avenue and 1st Street intersection. As one of the first banks in the city, it played a significant role in the city's success, with O.A. Fechter and George Donald both serving as the bank's presidents during its existence. Today, the lot is occupied by Key Bank. (Above, photograph by Spike and Company.)

In 1905, the Yakima Tea Company was located on the south side of East Yakima Avenue between 1st and 2nd Streets. At the time of the photograph to the left, Fred Thomas Briggs was the president of the company, with Lapier Voce Ballinger serving as the secretary. By 1908, the company had moved to South 2nd Street, and it made another move—to North 2nd Street—shortly afterward. Today, the location appears much different.

In the 1890s, the First National Bank was located at the southwest corner of East Yakima Avenue and 2nd Street, as shown below. Prior to the business being relocated to North Yakima, it was a wood building in Yakima City (now Union Gap). After serving as the home to the bank, the building housed several other businesses, including the Dudley Shoe Store. Later, it became the site of the Larson Building.

The Taft & Taft Building stood on the north side of East Yakima Avenue between 1st and 2nd Streets. In the 1901 photograph at left, the building was home to the S.O. Hawkes Jewelry company, which later relocated to the Yakima Trust Building. The Taft & Taft building no longer exists, and a portion of the lot is occupied by the east side of the Wells Fargo Bank.

STREET SCENES

In the 1890s street scene above, the North Yakima Milling Company is shown behind a group of Native Americans standing at the intersection of East Yakima Avenue and 2nd Street. The North Yakima Milling Company was located on the northeast corner of the intersection. The site later became home to the Miller Building, and today, it is occupied by the Wheatland Bank. (Above, photograph by Frank P. Lanterman.)

Occupying the northeast corner of East Yakima Avenue and 2nd Street, the Miller Building (below) was one of the city's larger buildings. When it was first constructed, it had five floors, and a sixth floor was added later, as shown in the photograph. The first floor housed several businesses, including the Cahalan Company, Dunbar & Nelson, and Pioneer Drug, all of which are visible in the below image. Today, the Wheatland Bank stands at the location.

The Ditter Brothers Clothing Store, started by Frank Ditter in Yakima City (now Union Gap), relocated to North Yakima (now Yakima) in 1888. Afterward, the business was given to Frank's sons Phil and Joe, who renamed it Ditter Brothers. In 1920, the store was located one lot east of the Miller Building on the north side of East Yakima Avenue. (Right, photograph by George Martin.)

Above is a westerly view of East Yakima Avenue between 2nd and 4th Streets in 1930. On the right, the W.E. Draper Inc. Store is visible at the northwest corner of 3rd Street, with the Miller Building behind it. Today, a Chase Bank occupies the location where Draper's once stood, and the Wheatland Bank replaced the Miller Building.

The above image looks west on East Yakima Avenue from west of 3rd Street in 1912. In this view, the Hotel Yakima is on the left, and the Bradbury Store, Ditter Brothers, and the Miller Building are on the right. Today, the Hotel Yakima and the buildings on the right side of the photograph no longer exist. (Above, photograph by Frank P. Lanterman.)

The Col. J.J. Weisenberger statue is shown in front of a Coffin Brothers Store at the intersection of East Yakima Avenue and 3rd Street in the 1907 image below. The statue, which was dedicated to the fallen of Company E in the Spanish-American War, was later moved twice. The Coffin Brothers Store shown was one of several of the business's locations. Today, a different building stands at the corner. (Below, photograph from Lanterman, Hutchings, Newman Scrapbooks and courtesy of Patricia Parrish and Yakima Valley Museum.)

STREET SCENES

The Masonic Temple (the Great Western Building) is shown below shortly after completion in 1911. At that time, the building sat at the northwest corner of what was then a four-way intersection of East Yakima Avenue and 4th Street. The north leg of the intersection no longer exists. The building was listed in the National Register of Historic Places in 1996 and still stands. Today, a parking garage occupies the location of what was once North 4th Street.

Shown above is a 1913 westward view of East Yakima Avenue from east of 4th Street. In the right foreground is the Great Western Building, which served as the home of the Masonic Temple on the upper floors. Eventually, part of the building was incorporated within the Yakima Mall. Today, a boutique hotel and other various businesses are housed within the structure. (Above, photograph by Frank P. Lanterman.)

Early automobile dealers on East Yakima Avenue west of Naches Avenue are pictured above in 1930. On the right are the Sheane Auto Company, Voak-Marmon Company, and the Washington Auto Company. A Firestone and Texaco business is on the left. Today, none of the dealers still exist at the location, and the north side of the street is dominated by the former Yakima Mall buildings. (Above, photograph by Tarter.)

In 1910, the St. Michaels Episcopal Church, located at the southeast corner of East Yakima Avenue and Naches Avenue, looked much different than it does today. The church is the oldest standing building in Yakima, with its construction beginning in approximately 1885. Today, the entrance and the outside of the building have changed dramatically. (Below, photograph by Jim Newbill.)

In 1910, the Yakima Auto & Supply Company, a Ford dealership, was located on the south side of East Yakima Avenue between 4th Street and Naches Avenue, as shown below. At the time of the below photograph, Fred Chandler was the president of the company, with Lee Tittle serving as the secretary. Today, the building no longer exists, and the lot now serves as a parking lot near the Chinook Tower.

CHAPTER

THEATERS

A float advertising the movie *Transatlantic* is pictured outside the Capitol Theatre, which was showing the movie in 1930. Located on the east side of South 3rd Street, the theater was called the Loew's State Theater and Mercy's Theater prior to becoming the Capitol. The theater is still in operation today.

In the 1900 photograph above, the Switzer Opera House (on the right) and the old North Yakima City Hall appear to be the same structure. The two buildings are actually separate, with the opera house being constructed in 1890 and the city hall in 1889. Built by A.J. Switzer, this served as an opera house for a short time before becoming the home of other businesses and activities. Today, the building still stands. (Above, photograph by Frank P. Lanterman.)

Mason's Opera House was located on the east side of North 1st Street just north of East Yakima Avenue. The building served as the first Switzer Opera House prior to becoming Mason's Opera House. The 1901 photograph at left shows a partial view of the opera house, with Janeck's Pharmacy operating on the first floor. The building no longer exists, and the site now serves as a parking lot for the Wells Fargo Bank.

Built in 1900, Larson's Theater once sat at the northwest corner of North 2nd Street and East A Street (now Staff Sgt. Pendleton Way), as shown below. It reportedly could seat 1,000 people and had the largest auditorium in the state at the time it was constructed. It later became the Yakima Theater. The building no longer exists. Performance Park now occupies the lots where the theater once stood. (Below, photograph by Frank P. Lanterman.)

The Lyric Theater (shown directly behind the horses in the above image) was located on the west side of North 2nd Street between East Yakima Avenue and East A Street (now Staff Sgt. Pendleton Way). While operating from the location, the Lyric shared the building with the Yakima Tea Company and the Imperial Hotel. Over the past century, the location has been home to many businesses. Today, it houses the Second Street Grill restaurant.

The Yakima Theater building (originally the Empire Building) was located on the east side of South 2nd Street between East Yakima and East Chestnut Avenues. In approximately 1930, the building was transformed into the Yakima Theater. The 1931 photograph above shows banners on the building welcoming the Mercys home. At the time of the photograph, the theater was showing Charlie Chaplin's *City Lights*. The building no longer stands.

The Liberty Theater was originally located on South 3rd Street. In approximately 1920, it relocated to the south side of East Yakima Avenue between 3rd and 4th Streets. In the 1941 photograph at left, banners for the spring movie festival hang from the building to welcome visitors to Yakima. The featured movie at the time was *The Great Lie*, starring Bette Davis and George Brent. The Liberty Theater no longer exists.

THEATERS 59

Completed in 1920, this building initially opened as the Mercy's Theater, then became the Loew's State Theatre. Shortly afterward, it became the home of the Capitol Theatre. The below photograph shows the building when it was Loew's State Theater. At the time of the photograph, advertisements outside the doors promoted a continuous matinee and *The Saphead*. Today, the building still serves as the home of the Capitol Theatre. (Below, photograph by Tarter.)

CHAPTER 3

COURTHOUSES

In 1906, a crowd gathered on North 2nd Street to watch and help extinguish a fire at the Yakima County Courthouse. Burned beyond repair, the structure was lost. A larger courthouse was constructed at the same location to replace it. Today, the Yakima County Courthouse is still located on the southwest corner of 2nd Street and East B Street (now Martin Luther King Jr. Boulevard).

At right is an 1897 view of the first wooden Yakima County Courthouse in North Yakima. The courthouse was originally located in Yakima City (now Union Gap). In 1886, when North Yakima became the seat of Yakima County, the courthouse was relocated to the intersection of North 2nd Street and East B Street (now Martin Luther King Jr. Boulevard) in North Yakima. The courthouse was replaced after it burned down in 1906. Over the past century, the building has undergone several changes and additions.

Below is a 1903 northwest view of the Yakima County Courthouse from North 2nd Street. At the time of the photograph, the courthouse was decorated and ready for an address to be given by Pres. Teddy Roosevelt on May 25, 1903. Three years later, the wooden courthouse burned down. Today, a much larger and more modern courthouse stands at the intersection of North 2nd Street and East B Street. (Below, photograph by Frank P. Lanterman.)

The below image looks south on North 2nd Street from East B Street (now Martin Luther King Jr. Boulevard) in 1906. On the right side of the photograph, the first Yakima County Courthouse in North Yakima is in the foreground, and the Larson Theater is visible in the background. The present-day Yakima County Courthouse building is larger, and the Larson Theater no longer exists. (Below, photograph by Frank P. Lanterman.)

The second Yakima County Courthouse in North Yakima is pictured above in 1910. The cornerstone for the second courthouse was laid at the intersection of North 2nd Street and East B Street (now Martin Luther King Jr. Boulevard) in June 1906. The memorial statue of J.J. Weisenberger, originally located at the intersection of 3rd Street and East Yakima Avenue, is standing in front of the courthouse. Today's Yakima County Courthouse is entirely different.

Above is a 1920 southwest view of the second Yakima County Courthouse with a cannon and the J.J. Weisenberger statue (on the left side of the image, behind the automobiles) in front of the courthouse. Not long after this picture was taken, the Weisenberger statue was moved to the intersection of Naches Avenue and East Yakima Avenue. The modern courthouse has changed significantly and has no front lawn.

The Yakima County Jail Bull Pen is shown below at the rear of the Yakima County Courthouse in 1933. The structure was used as part of the county jail until its destruction around 1950. A newer Bull Pen was attached to the county courthouse for use by the county jail. Today, the site of the old Bull Pen serves as a parking lot for the Yakima County Courthouse.

COURTHOUSES

Below is a 1920 photograph of the US Post Office and Courthouse located at the northeast corner of South 3rd Street and East Chestnut Avenue. Built in 1912, this served as both the post office and federal courthouse until the post office was relocated. In 1978, the building was renamed the William O. Douglas US Courthouse and Federal Building, in honor of the Yakima native. Today, the building still serves as the federal courthouse.

In February 1940, work was being done on the US Post Office and Courthouse. This 1940 photograph, signed (on the back of the image) by A. Earl Patterson, the construction engineer, served as a form of documentation for the work being completed by contractor Eivind Anderson on the north side of the building. It is now known as the William O. Douglas US Courthouse and Federal Building.

Courthouses

In May 1912, the US Post Office and Courthouse was near completion. This view of rear east side of the building shows the final stages of construction. Two of the city's larger hotels, the Donnelly and the Commercial, are visible in the background. Located on the northeast corner of South 3rd Street and East Chestnut Avenue, this building still stands and is surrounded by other familiar landmarks, including the Capitol Theatre.

CHAPTER 4

FIRE STATIONS

A North Yakima Fire Department chemical truck is pictured in front of Fire Station No. 2 in 1914. After relocating from its original site within the Old North Yakima City Hall on North Front Street prior to 1910, the fire department had two stations, with Fire Station No. 2 being located at 16 North 4th Street. (Photograph by Frank P. Lanterman.)

Built in 1898, the old North Yakima City Hall building is located on the east side of North Front Street between East Yakima Avenue and East A Street (now Staff Sgt. Pendleton Way). The building served as the home of the city's fire department, police department, jail, and city offices until approximately 1908. In the photograph at right, the front doors of the fire department are shown with horse-drawn fire equipment inside the building. Although it is still standing, the building looks significantly different today.

Below, a North Yakima Fire Department horse-drawn fire engine and its crew are pictured outside the first North Yakima Fire Department. Originally located within the old North Yakima City Hall on the east side of North Front Street, the department relocated in approximately 1909 when the building was deemed unfit and unsanitary. Today, the structure still stands, although it has undergone several changes.

Above, North Yakima Fire Department equipment and personnel are shown exiting the front doors of the North Yakima Fire Department headquarters and Fire Station No. 1 in 1914. Located on South 3rd Street at the northeast corner of the East Walnut Street intersection, this served as one of the two fire stations in the city at the time. Today, the building is home to a pawn shop. (Above, photograph by Frank P. Lanterman.)

FIRE STATIONS

CHAPTER 5

HOTELS

The Hotel Yakima was located at the southwest corner of South 3rd Street and East Yakima Avenue in 1890. This was one of the first hotels in the city after it was moved from Yakima City (now Union Gap). Its upper porch served as a popular viewing location during local events. (Courtesy of Click Relander collection and Yakima Valley Museum.)

Located at 322 West Yakima Avenue, the Savoy Hotel was once a popular west-side hotel. In 1913, when the below photograph was taken, Harry Sommerville, who lived at the Savoy, was the hotel's proprietor. Over the last century, the building has housed a variety of businesses as well as apartments on the upper floors. Today, the building is vacant. The below image first appeared in the North Yakima High School yearbook, the *Wigwam*.

Located at the southeast corner of North Front Street and East A Street (now Staff Sgt. Pendleton Way), the Sydney Hotel was built by Julia Hess in 1910. The building contained the hotel on the upper floors and businesses like that of the Sydney Saloon on the first floor. Its location—across from the North Yakima Train Depot—helped to assure the hotel's success. Today, the building has apartments on its upper floors.

HOTELS

The Michigan Hotel building stands on the southwest corner of North 1st Street and East A Street (now Staff Sgt. Pendleton Way). While the hotel was on the upper floors, businesses such as a bar and a barbershop were located on the first floor. Built by Patrick Mullins, the Michigan was his third hotel in the city. Today, the upper floors of the building serve as apartments, while the first floor houses various businesses.

Built in 1889 to replace the original wood structure that was moved from Yakima City (now Union Gap), the second Hotel Bartholet (shown below) was one of the first hotels in the city. Located on the west side of North 1st Street between East Yakima Avenue and East A Street (now Staff Sgt. Pendleton Way), the hotel was owned by the Bartholet family. It offered a stagecoach for transport to the train depot. The building was demolished in 1989; the site is now a parking lot.

The Hotel Washington (shown below) sat at the northwest corner of East Yakima Avenue and North 1st Street in 1913. Built by Patrick Mullins, the hotel incorporated the existing Schott Brothers structure when it was constructed. After the property burned down in 1970, a restaurant replaced the hotel building. Today, the site is home to a McDonald's.

In 1915, the Kentucky Home Boarding House was located on the east side of North 1st Street between East A Street (now Staff Sgt. Pendleton Way) and East B Street (now Martin Luther King Jr. Boulevard). It was a boardinghouse type of hotel and was run by several women over time. Alice E. Larson operated the business in 1908, charging 50¢ per day for a furnished room. Today, the site is part of the south parking lot for the Yakima County Courthouse.

HOTELS

155- First Street, North Yakima, Washington.

The above postcard looks north on South 1st Street toward East Yakima Avenue. The Pacific Hotel (foreground) and the Washington Hotel (background) are on the left side of the image. Both hotels were operational at the same time, competing with one another for business. The Pacific Hotel was located within what was once the city's Japan Town, while the Washington Hotel was across East Yakima Avenue. Today, only the Pacific Hotel building remains standing.

The structure shown below was erected in 1903 as a two-story building, and a third floor was added in 1906. Located within what was once the city's Japan Town, the 60-room Pacific Hotel, which operated inside the building, became well-known when George and Koto Hirahara purchased the business in 1926. The Hiraharas successfully operated the hotel until the evacuation of Japanese Americans during World War II. Today, the building houses businesses on the first floor. (Below, courtesy of the Hirahara Family Collection, Yakima Valley Museum.)

The Guilland Hotel was originally located in Yakima City (now Union Gap). Owned by David and Marie Guilland, it was one of the first buildings moved to North Yakima (now Yakima). It took approximately a month to move the hotel before it was finally placed at the northwest corner of the South 1st Street and East Chestnut Avenue intersection. The hotel was later replaced with the Montana Hotel, constructed by Pat Mullins. Today, both buildings are gone, and a parking lot has replaced them.

Built in 1908 by brothers Judd and Grant Elliott, the Hotel Tieton was located at the southeast corner of South 1st Street and East Chestnut Avenue. From 1954 to the mid-1970s, the hotel was owned by members of the Benny Kwong family, as was the Dragon Inn Restaurant that opened inside the building in 1964. Together, the two businesses were among the last to exist in what was once the city's Chinatown, with the restaurant closing in 1994. The building is now home to renovated apartments and other businesses.

The Donnelly Hotel was located on the east side of South 2nd Street between East Yakima and East Chestnut Avenues. In 1910, the building housed the Eastern Furniture Store on the first floor. Prior to being named the Donnelly, it was called the Strand Hotel, the Hotel Locke, and the Grand Hotel. After serving as the Donnelly, it changed to the Chieftain Hotel. Today, the building is gone, and the site contains a parking lot.

The Yakima Hotel (below) was located at the southwest corner of 3rd Street and East Yakima Avenue. Originally a wood structure, the hotel was moved from Yakima City (now Union Gap) in the 1880s and rebuilt and then remodeled several times after the move. Between 1903 and 1909 (around the time the below photograph was taken), it was a popular hotel in the city and had an upper deck for visitors to watch street activity and view the J.J. Weisenberger memorial statue located in the middle of the intersection. About a century after the time of the below image, the hotel building was demolished and replaced with an Olive Garden.

The Commercial Hotel was located on the south side of East Yakima Avenue just east of 3rd Street. In the 1913 photograph below, the three buildings associated with the hotel are visible; Reading's Pharmacy operated from the first floor of the building. J.M. Hitchings lived at the hotel and served as its manager at the time. Today, the buildings still stand, and the upper floors house apartments. (Below, photograph by Frank P. Lanterman.)

CHAPTER 6

TRAIN DEPOTS

The arrival of the railroad in the Yakima Valley was the reason that North Yakima (now Yakima) began in 1884. The first passenger train depot in the city was a wooden boxcar placed in the middle of what is now East Yakima Avenue at Front Street. By the time this 1908 photograph was taken, a third passenger train depot (visible behind the train) had been placed on the north side of the street to allow for east and west travel on East Yakima Avenue.

In the May 1894 photograph above, members of Coxey's Army are shown waiting outside the second North Yakima passenger train depot en route to Washington, DC, for a labor protest. After the photograph was taken, a riot occurred at the site. In the background of the photograph is the second North Yakima passenger depot, which was built in 1886. (Above, photograph by L.E. Smith; courtesy of Kooser and Yakima Valley Museum.)

The railroad properties surrounding the various train depots in the city were once bustling with activity, including the unloading of Ringling Bros. Circus wagons along North Front Street, as shown in the 1901 image below. In the background of the photograph are a number of fruit row buildings. Today, this location is home to a parking lot. (Below, photograph by Frank P. Lanterman; courtesy of the Jack Whitnall Collection and Yakima Valley Museum.)

The third North Yakima Northern Pacific Railroad depot is pictured below at the northwest corner of East Yakima Avenue and Front Street. Built in 1898, the structure was much larger than the previous two depots and the first to not sit in the middle of East Yakima Avenue. It served as the passenger train depot until 1910, when the fourth depot was completed. Today, the building that sits on the lot appears much different.

The crowd shown above gathered at the intersection of North Front Street and Yakima Avenue, outside the third train depot, to await the arrival of Pres. Teddy Roosevelt on May 25, 1903. After he got into town, President Roosevelt participated in a parade down East Yakima Avenue, gave a public speech, and was then escorted back to the depot for his departure. (Above, photograph by Frank P. Lanterman; courtesy of the Jack Whitnall Collection and Yakima Valley Museum.)

TRAIN DEPOTS   93

Above, a group is shown posing in front of the south side of the fourth Yakima passenger train depot in 1930. Construction on the fourth depot was completed in 1910. The building still stands at the intersection of North Front Street and Staff Sgt. Pendleton Way. Passenger train service no longer exists in Yakima, but North Town Coffee and a restaurant currently conduct business from inside the building.

The back (west side) of the fourth passenger train depot in North Yakima is pictured below in 1910, shortly after it was constructed to meet the increasing size of the city. The south side of the building also served as the location for the Yakima Commercial Club Fruit Stand. The historic depot remains standing and is now home to businesses. (Below, photograph by Frank P. Lanterman.)

TRAIN DEPOTS

Discover Thousands of Local History Books
Featuring Millions of Vintage Images

Arcadia Publishing, the leading local history publisher in the United States, is committed to making history accessible and meaningful through publishing books that celebrate and preserve the heritage of America's people and places.

Find more books like this at
www.arcadiapublishing.com

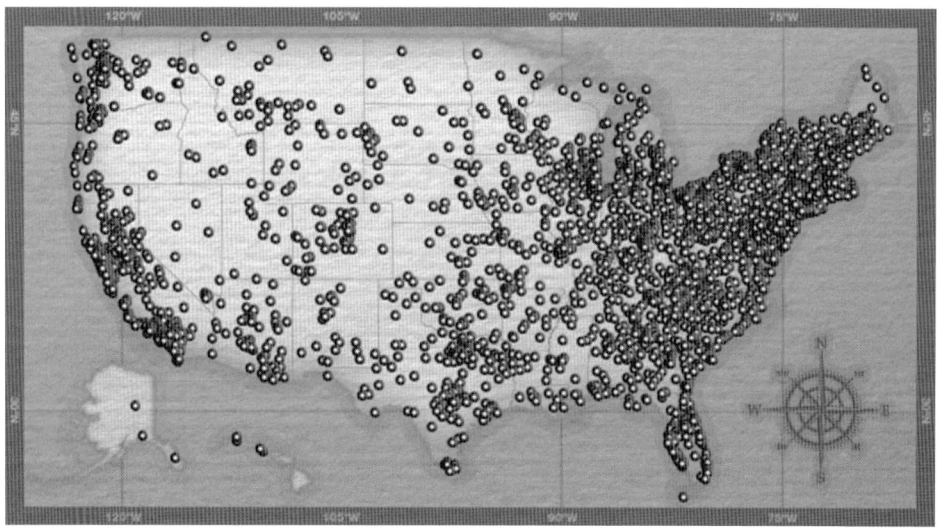

Search for your hometown history, your old stomping grounds, and even your favorite sports team.

Consistent with our mission to preserve history on a local level, this book was printed in South Carolina on American-made paper and manufactured entirely in the United States. Products carrying the accredited Forest Stewardship Council (FSC) label are printed on 100 percent FSC-certified paper.